# IT'S TIME TO EAT GREEN APPLES

# It's Time to Eat
# GREEN APPLES

## Walter the Educator

Silent King Books
A WhichHead Entertainment Imprint

Copyright © 2025 by Walter the Educator

All rights reserved. No part of this book may be reproduced in any manner whatsoever without written per- mission except in the case of brief quotations embodied in critical articles and reviews.

First Printing, 2024

Disclaimer

This book is a literary work; the story is not about specific persons, locations, situations, and/or circumstances unless mentioned in a historical context. Any resemblance to real persons, locations, situations, and/or circumstances is coincidental. This book is for entertainment and informational purposes only. The author and publisher offer this information without warranties expressed or implied. No matter the grounds, neither the author nor the publisher will be accountable for any losses, injuries, or other damages caused by the reader's use of this book. The use of this book acknowledges an understanding and acceptance of this disclaimer.

It's Time to Eat GREEN APPLES is a collectible early learning book by Walter the Educator suitable for all ages belonging to Walter the Educator's Time to Eat Book Series. Collect more books at WaltertheEducator.com

**USE THE EXTRA SPACE TO TAKE NOTES AND DOCUMENT YOUR MEMORIES**

# GREEN APPLES

It's time to eat, oh what a treat!

# It's Time to Eat

# Green Apples

A crunchy snack that's crisp and sweet.

Shiny, bright, and full of fun,

A green apple for everyone!

Pick it up and take a bite,

Juicy, tart, and fresh, just right!

It makes a crunch, oh, what a sound!

A yummier fruit can't be found!

Green apples grow up big and round,

On trees so tall above the ground.

The farmers pick them one by one,

Then send them out for apple fun!

Slice them up or eat them whole,

In your lunch or in a bowl.

Pack one up to take to school,

A snack like this is super cool!

# It's Time to Eat

# Green Apples

They help you grow up strong and bright,

Giving you energy and might.

For running, jumping, work, or play,

A green apple powers your day!

Some taste sour, some taste sweet,

But every one's a tasty treat.

Dip in yogurt, honey too,

There are so many things to do!

A rainbow snack is fun to try,

Red and green stacked way up high!

Mix with berries, grapes, and more,

Fruit is never ever a bore!

Baked in pies or made in sauce,

Apples win, they're never lost!

But fresh and crunchy, all can see,

## It's Time to Eat

# Green Apples

That's the best way it should be!

So grab a green one, big and round,

The yummiest fruit that can be found.

Take a bite, so crisp, so neat,

A green apple can't be beat!

It's time to eat, let's take a seat,

A snack that's healthy, fresh, and sweet.

A green apple, oh what fun,

It's Time to Eat

# Green Apples

Crunch, munch, and now we're done!

# ABOUT THE CREATOR

Walter the Educator is one of the pseudonyms for Walter Anderson. Formally educated in Chemistry, Business, and Education, he is an educator, an author, a diverse entrepreneur, and he is the son of a disabled war veteran. "Walter the Educator" shares his time between educating and creating. He holds interests and owns several creative projects that entertain, enlighten, enhance, and educate, hoping to inspire and motivate you. Follow, find new works, and stay up to date with Walter the Educator™

at WaltertheEducator.com

www.ingramcontent.com/pod-product-compliance
Lightning Source LLC
LaVergne TN
LVHW052012060526
838201LV00059B/3992